Spleen Elegy

JASON LABBE

BLAZEVOX[BOOKS]
Buffalo, New York

Spleen Elegy
by Jason Labbe

Copyright © 2017

Published by BlazeVOX [books]

Printed in the United States of America

Interior design and typesetting by Geoffrey Gatza
Cover art and interior images by Melanie Willhide
Cover design by Michelle Lee
Author portrait by Brad Amorosino

First Edition
ISBN: 978-1-60964-298-3
Library of Congress Control Number: 2017947135

BlazeVOX [books]
131 Euclid Ave
Kenmore, NY 14217
Editor@blazevox.org

publisher of weird little books

BlazeVOX [books]

blazevox.org

21 20 19 18 17 16 15 14 13 12 01 02 03 04 05 06 07 08 09 10

BlazeVOX

Contents

Stitches

After Infection

Bethany Dusk Radio

Spleen Elegy

Stitches

Half-Life in the Half-Light

In spring snow it's difficult to believe, a bone
broken for each year alive instantly
maxing out wallets of credit cards. I couldn't tell you
the colors of emergency surgery, I can't recall
signing next to the X—because I never—
and so promise to mispronounce *pre-certification.*
I still pause before my name as though asked
by a stranger in a dream to approach
a black band of water at dusk. The day
I glimpsed my X-ray of eighteen broken ribs
I plotted to walk the thawing canal, to repeat
that trail—it's absurd—where a sign warns against
approaching hostile swans nesting.
                          Today I hike through
a squall, and without a hood, my head open
to the buds and blossoms in shock. I receive a sky
more static than grey, white noise of wind and vapor.
I count eighteen sticks snap under my left steps,
and I'm home. My fingers numb, I fumble
with the light dimmer, then the stereo volume,
and with eyes half-closed up my dosage
of low frequencies, bass in the chest.
Check below the ache in my sternum: I slept
through the stitches and woke to a foot-long scar
no one can tell me how I'll pay for. What could I do
but steal the scalpel. Now no traffic light halo, no
rise in barometric pressure, and no path of black

ice can strand me. This improvised power ballad
whose words the world must understand
loops in my head, around my apartment, around
the building, rides off the whitening curb, and laps
the block before skidding into a parked delivery truck.
But the instrumental version blows straight out
of the city and spreads into a colder fringe where
my future house glows behind rows of grey trees.

Later, in the Black-Eyed Susans

It's not how but where.

*

Yellow stipples the roadside,
the hill. One sign warns of falling rocks,
another of deer crossing.

Another mile and the fear
of flying, which is not to say vertigo.
At the next stoplight
a landing plane flies over, low,
and interrupts reception.
"Hello Goodbye" comes back on
two beats behind where you expect it.

*

It's not when but where.

Some mornings the surrounding mountains loom.
When paramedics cut off your hiking boots
vertigo began.

*

The two times worth waiting for:
later, too late.
The first is here, the other—

*

Nowhere is near last year's dream:
you flew from the truck
and lay beside a Triumph Tiger.
Or was it vice versa?
Find both ways to say
"I was bleeding to death on the side of the road."

Tattoo Removal

"Get comfortable," our man said to her,
gun in hand. This was for the Daisy,

a decade before the Black Bird
and Mountain Laurel up my shoulder—
a view designed to brighten
my recurring dream
of the world through a broken windshield:

my motorcycle sliding away on its side,
its shattered turn signals,
the front wheel still spinning.

The Daisy on her leg is fading.

The rider is vanishing.

                    *

The Daisy wasn't dark enough to begin with.

It needs three more sessions
with the clinical laser. The Daisy will never completely disappear.

When it fades as much as it might
she will go back to our man
for a white heart
with a red spot in the center. On her chest.

*

I woke in my truck with a broken nose,
a shattered hand,
and her inexplicably asleep
in the other seat. Glass
in my lap and around my feet.

Something had torn her Daisy.

We were deep in the mountain laurel, a branch-tip was reaching
through the passenger window.
I wanted bunches
of blossoms. Never her blood
or the ambulance.

The radio was still on. It couldn't have been a song.

Each petal was the size of a thumbnail,
white and flecked red.

*

"Get comfortable," our man said to me.
This was for the Bird and the Laurel.
When I placed my drink of water
on his drawing table he dipped his gun,
rinsed out the black ink. "Take a sip."
He snickers. Our man shades.

20

*

When the Daisy has faded as much as it might
she will ask me
to count the little light hairs and freckles
around the abstract scar.

I will trace the Heart with my thumb.

A Reception, a Garage, Mountains North and South

The left end of an ornate table, the far
right side of the photo, my gaze
in the teacup held to my face.
She has one eye on the centerpiece.
I shape and reshape the half of her
out of frame, the side of her easing away
no matter where the picture hangs.
Oil drips from the crank case broke open.
One drop follows the next,
and the spot on the driveway grows.
Mountains blue all around
are nothing like last year's—
northern and cut with roads she knew.
The late shadow, third gear,
was like another us
gliding over the rough roadside.
She dug her chin into my shoulder,
and her untied hair flew straight back.
My torso is forgetting her hold.
The oil spot grows. A drop
could melt her Berkshire snow.
Down on a couch in the South
I thank Appalachia she stayed
states away, that I crashed
without a passenger, that my body alone
broke open the body of the bike.
My vintage chrome. In the North, enamored,

she gestured as if with a camera.
She feared the interstate. It thrilled her.
With one week left of midnight rides
we wagered when our friends would separate.
We lose either way. One drop, two,
I lie still so the graft will take.
My sutures are beautiful as a tread pattern.
The day I am off my back I will scour the town
for the truck, the scratched and gouged
bumper that matches my dents.
I will kiss the fuck who hit me.
I am building a great garage.
The bones are in place.
I will tear down my salvaged machine,
leave no part attached to another.
I will devise a way to straighten the frame
and find a period-correct, patina-perfect
replacement for each bent or broken part.
I will rebuild with no pillion position.
Above a mess of tools and workshop manuals,
the photo: Dessert At The Reception.
It could take weeks to perfect
the electrics. When I read the word
wound in the wiring diagram, a map
almost too difficult to follow, I will remember
the smell of blood on the street.
I will mount
a headlight sharp and bright as a bullet.

Metal Heart

I was full of jealousy and oranges.
One was fuel, the other out of season.

I was on my motorcycle and third gear
had spread a glaze of ice across the city.

Hard on the throttle and up-shifting,
I had sun in the rearview. But all I wanted

was a tighter corner in fourth, another hour
without sleeping, a single evening oblivious

to traffic signals and a bus's slow skid
toward the guardrail. Winter never gives

good oranges or traction in a hairpin.
No market was near enough, or tropical.

The Boulevard wasn't cold enough, and no
passenger could handle fifth, a climax

worth some grey in my beard. My left eye.
I was full of bluster, revving out, growing leaner

so as to ergonomically fit the machine
that wanted to injure me. I was neither tired

nor hungry. Daylight suspended in cloud,
orange glow sinking behind the city.

I was hard on the throttle and out of gears.
What was that beating under my jacket.

Solo

Hard on the throttle in third the rider traced the white center line. Blasting along back routes through pitch black was a private posterity when he'd take a tight blind right pushing sixty. The point was to muscle the motorcycle into a severe lean, hang a hip inside, touch footrest to pavement, lightly. To leave behind a faint smear of rubber nobody would see. The point was precision. There was no moon and so no high beam. The exhaust note spread into vague meadows and jagged black tree clusters. The exhaust note entered houses whose lights turned on or didn't.

*

She lost interest in her club soda, excused herself from a conversation about recent heat and humidity. She touched up her lipstick without a mirror, one smooth curving motion. Touched bottom lip to top, then left him one last message. Dropped her phone into her purse and something broke.

*

Losing the town at your back, restaurants and theatres full of couples. Full of lights. The road narrowed again, wound through blackening woods. Arrival, a clearing, was not the point. Focus was not thinking about the point. Focus was watching the roadside ditch for a shift, for glowing eyes. Something that could tangle with the front wheel and bend spokes like grass.

*

How could the party miss him. The rider believed the harder he rode the less he would be remembered. And she believed her every exhale pressured an object. Moved it. Fleck of dust, a finger, a machine of metal. She imagined herself a tailwind.

*

The rider was attempting to weave a breeze through an invisible tree. Without disturbing a single twig or leaf. He accelerated hard out of a tight left. Every turn was away.

Blue Note

Because there is only interval quiet,
the impossibility of silence
even after midnight, I am reaching
for a distant tone: a single word, a sum
of melody and rhythm in their absence.
Clouds with glowing edges suggest
extension. Inaudible dust and moths
hovering around the floodlight offer
suspension. If I say sound alone
comprises song, which supposes
location, the committee of crickets asserts
intention. Great jazz only happens
in hard-hitting cities, another era.
Even minor sidemen knew that
to build a ballad you must
shape heartbreak, mimic the ostinato
of heart-pump and bloodflow, know
when to release a slow
brushstroke across the snare drum.
When to surrender a breath.
Night air streams in place of daylight.
A new variation of tired smells—
mown grass, a neighbor's faint cigarette,
my perspiration—insists *recollection*.
I was raised in the past but couldn't stay.
It's perfectly fine to be consoled
by a three-chord cliché, to circle

the darkening blocks until
your knees ache like the overplayed
pop song you can't name or forget.
The far-off dog barking is never a stray.
This is no route through, this is not
a destination—and so the record collection
expands, the shelf sags lower.
The best jackets involve sad, beautiful
faces viewed through some blue lens.
Every blues is a plea for that face to stay.
The last window glowing blue goes dark.
This late pain is a light
metallic taste I want to vibrate, though
dedicating one's life to mastering
an instrument attempts *possession*.
This guitar's as good as stolen.
I have scratched my name inside.
I own its mahogany body but not its tone.

Waltz for Debby

I said to the woman
in Lenscrafters make me
sound like Bill Evans, flatter

my grainy portrait, allow
me his wild horse—
white and shining calm or

darkening and utterly
unbreakable. Accompany me
with brushes on a cymbal,

walk an unbroken bass line
while I limp toward bird
tracks, stitches in last

night's light snow.
I see your name
is Debby. I'm listening.

The Orgasm as Minor Failure

No war has ever been won in drowsiness
though many brilliant inventions first appear
as a metallic spill not a puddle on your otherwise

clear table of half-sleep. Most often the spill
not a puddle will evaporate come sunrise.
Daybreak is a vacancy the exact dimensions

of your full name. The name you left behind
the shed on a blanket in the wet grass. Behind
the Boys' Club on a bus in the parking lot.

You lose and find your name countless times.
On a blanket in the yard on a bus in the lot.
Consult every man you know no matter

how unapproachable—your father
or imaginary brother—and it's unanimous:
bleakness is the blanket of your favorite color

contrasted by grey pavement surrounding
the lustrous puddle that never reflects you.
The puddle that reappears every morning after.

Oar

Driving further into dusk seldom brings me far
from the canal you call a river, farther from the vision
of white-robed women. Seldom beyond them

or morning I was not quite waking. An unfamiliar
finger finessed the volume and the face above
watched my eyelids to adjust accordingly. I love

your mother for her gift, that small radio. Tonight
my fingers draw over car stereo controls. Another drive
north, evening repeats an actual coast.

*

A drive along the water deeper into forest offered
a new plan, away from/closer to constant mountains,
the severest blue. I heard reverb surround guitars,

dark in the branches. There was a palm
on the gear shift; the face above spotted the tree
and we skidded accordingly into the local paper.

My palm glides over my sorest ribs, the crosshatch
of scars. Another morning drive delayed
covers a lower altitude, another alternate route.

*

The hive we avoid determines the one we enter.
The door opens to a walk that leads to a turkey vulture
picking at a road kill opossum. When I hear an owl

I cannot see him, when a female cardinal
is at the feeder I watch morning showers draw on
and warm into everything germinating. I rake

like my father, I await him in his pickup. Another
perfectionist would procrastinate in this weather.
But no haul pushed off clears a storm's debris.

                    *

Dark on the canal. Under the hive my stung hand swells.
Have the family diamond, each decade a weakened
prong or scratch on the band. The women I dreamed

I do not see. With little to say about the swelling
the face above, no longer unfamiliar, offers
a pleasant chill. You put the ring to my cheek

and my finger is on the volume. A white robe
is a kind of barrier. I am awake—I take mine off
and shiver. The river shines for me.

Blackwash Canal

Where

From the hotel window above the courtyard
                    one might not miss the pool
      or the canal
      for that matter
If one were to search for disappearance this
would not be the leap

      *

We could drive out to the northwest corner
where the roads get confusing and follow
instinct into a mountain We would not notice
our bodies thrown
upon themselves and each other

      *

                  at which point I could say
I am addicted to little

When sleep took on too raw a texture
I thought *call me* and our shame may vanish
I was not woken

There was little to do at night but
drive the outskirts

*

If your ring never slipped into the pond
If a puddle could only be circled from its center

If the accumulation of fieldstones
didn't cause the wall's intensity

If the street didn't facilitate the trespasser
If I'd never driven by and admired the horse

If it were not the practice of the addict
to pay/beg for a strange bed in which to withdraw

If you knew the practice of the insomniac
If practice knew only the desired result

If your ring never dropped from the rowboat
and I drove us home without headlights

Dawn was when
there is no then

*

There is little to drive some nights but the canal
rushing
Quiet is as
close as I get

to a pond

that other town

where the craving can but does not dissolve

Each strip moved along
or across is a shining blackwash

What

the left hand that itches to introduce
a warmth
to the side of a horse

the pasture daily driven past

by the right hand as an extension
of grass
and the infinitesimal divide
of touch

the grass as measure of sky
or the degree of green
in the brown horse's mystique

further and farther across the fields
hang stars hardly watched
by the city where

no starlight falls on a cooling hand
and
there is no affectionate animal only

what takes and takes until
your call
the warmth

tonight does not deserve

obscures the swirl
the print on the hotel sill

Why

your hair is damp
black in the picture
thin snow on the slick steps
and anticipating rain
the conversation already
emptied and the truck
loaded with approaching
spring's junk

no ledge ever high enough
to talk us down
without the ring did you think
the nickel is lost
and the dime
sure to be discovered
you are so surprisingly
tall and always lovely

a week away renews
the distance this mood
depends on every edge
of the city I visit
softening through wayfarers
allow me another
encounter with your stature
that windy effect

How

With one hand behind my back
and the other ready
                to coast toward my side
of our epic duet sung
across an indescribable boundary
Or

for you I'll remain
                stationary and awake
in the decision the difficulty the

parapet
the quiet around the window

                *

With a record playing
with rolling drums rolling me
I don't fucking care
I exhale on the upbeats

                *

Via the elevator that rises out of the hotel
Pretending we
can climb so many flights is

impossible
The railing can't save us

*

In another picture
you are hilarious
with the indescribable way you shape
                    a past of little use
around that contorted face

So many visible ways to say *need*
and always mean it

When

Between waking and never,
the pasture only cattle graze.
The delusion of the horse
is another way to say ghost.
I wake with the feeling not the image.

Every night I spend driving the outskirts
comes before the church service,
a morning of visible rain.
Where I will travel the weather
does not follow. South is sunny

and your phone off or eaten
by the bottom of the canal.
Tomorrow is *your* answer,
my best suit pressed and laid out.
Do not imagine the mites in the creases.

Who(m)

what else but waking
to your face and fluorescent corona
wearing dark frames new enough
not to have appeared before

what else but waking
to you reading a magazine
to me a sort of blurry sister

what else but waking
again the curtains drawn
or a wall grown across
the window
near some surface far from sterile
transport to infection

the syringe you could not bear
the book you could not bring
the narcotized
whom you could not locate
what else but the window was
concealed a line around
your forehead

what else but straight above
what else but not quite dead
what else was waking again

After Infection

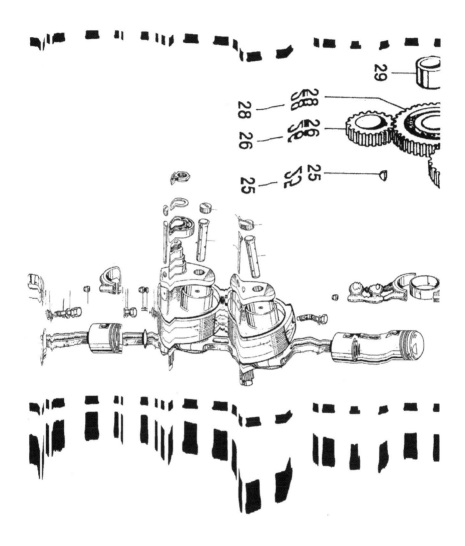

29

28 28 28
28 26 26 26
26

25 25 25
25

After Infection

To forget the year of fevers.
To enter warm air, endless
pathogens. Nothing sterile. The skin

not so much a barrier
as a membrane
the mild breeze blows through.

A decasecond of dusk is enough.
Swollen sun coming down,
the turkey vulture's swoop

behind the pines on the outskirts, all
above moving closer to some
out-of-view point of ground.

To watch. To forget
the Era of Lost Sleep
after the promised guest never showed.

A thin sweat is enough.

If a Train

Not a wall but the surface across which the room
is projected. Warmth and light and radio static
surround your shadow—picture a winter finch's tracks,
stitches in snow, last February's hold.
Here we cannot pass without outline or distinction.
And if a train were possible it would seem to float
from the trees behind the block, pass through
either window, either wound, and arrive
restless once we are dreaming. But things seldom enter
our sleep and some small part of a waking plan,
the way a droning coal train or a robin lifting out of a bath
can inhabit a passage in the pianist's improvisation
or the assassin's choice of socks (red)
on a morning too misty for truth in his aim.
If a train were possible the metaphors, the figures—
the projections—would have to collapse.
We'd call things what they are and question
our sense of direction in the life-size atlas.
Not a wall but a plain, a vastness, leading to an abrupt
horizon, where the room's focus shifts: not a door
so much as a feeling of starting out, the impetus
for painting the inside surface cumulonimbus in sunset.
A notion of distance. Plum was too earthy
for your form never fumbling with the glass knob,
a sort of early star. Pass with me following, closely,
into *outside*, innocuous misnomer that will facilitate
our escape. We'll wind through a series of woods

and clearings toward anonymity: sidewalks shining
at windows, all things below sky shining back.
We'll leave the vehicle for thieves
to strip and burn, we will walk into a nightlife
of gorgeous mistakes. By way of heat rising over asphalt,
feet lifting from that rougher surface
—nowhere to *live*—the sanguinity unfolding
inside a new city. If a train were possible we could stay.

To Find the Shape Before the Name

The street ends before the tracks
and the tracks bend
behind the black only trees can make.
Now streetlight corrupts us. The shadow
of another freight train
streams across the side of the white shed.
It's not that night begins
in the middle of something—
point of departure,

                     a suggestion of distance,
is a way to say nothing nowhere.

    *

Few would beg for life on the porch.
Few would refuse it:

                    back yard of shadow, blue
light of slipping hours, her asleep
          against me—the twitch
from her untouchable dream.
Is there a name for this

shape, or only description.

    *

The train brakes and steel tons screech
like some kind of agony.
                    The reappearing
moon's corona makes it easy for her
to think of a massive machine
as a *suffering childish beast.*

Stars are not so steely.

                    *

I never wonder where it's going, only why
it keeps coming through here.

                    *

We want to find the concealed cry
as much as we want
                    to run from it.

Dusk below the old trestle
                    we found in the gravel
little bleached bones scattered around
a column of vertebrae.
I almost scooped them onto a cold thin scrap
of rusty tin.

Light humidity holds night together.
Asleep against me she is warm and oily.

Moth Light

The twilight landscape comes on
and one channel of a thousand lights the window.
A glowing eye peering out exposes

the thicket. What national affair fails to intrude
on frost coming over crickets
in the back yard that smoothes over

the nearby city talking over water levels rising.
Or is your warming anxiety landlocked,
a product, and the cartography fixed.

Witness the interior turned in further
by the flat screen displaying
itself and a big budget crash scene or

a reporter's apology for the interruption.
All the words mean *something happened*
at the center of the dying insects.

Locate where *all the fading fireflies* go
after summer around your satellite dish—
oil tanker, Blackhawk rotor blade, drone wing.

The new fixture in which no wing burns
in vain is a derisory dream, *alternative fact*,
unless a whiter bulb shines above

the door. Beyond the yard beyond the window
whose hand holds yours,
who will grab the wheel if you nod off,

where will the moth go tonight

Return to the Canal

Interior Talk Radio

Find the station not of static
but translucence. Name it.
Lock the dial, walk
backward, canal-bound.

There is nothing left
to believe in or
want but everything,
and no dead air is standing.

Tune into what slides
out of place—rotten tomato,
book you should not read,
rusting Cadillac. Dwell in that report,

extend your neck for better reception.
Beckon the brother
you didn't hear vanish
and broadcast his name.

Maybe a decade will assuage
the grief that thrives
in distance. He was never born
to sand in Baghdad.

Fox in the Road

If you can forget
what he said say it
again. The process
begins in a glare—

the tepid green water stalls.
If you lose the cause.
In his dying car, air off.
The water, the road,

beside each other.
Listen, you are *there*
with dusk
when a fox comes out

of the brush to cross
where?—into traffic
is so obvious.
Never too good for despair,

if you remember
one thing he believed
baby say it twice in a whisper
and with sunglasses on.

Then Eighteen Blank Pages

In his diary (close it)
a distant grey road (drive away)—
sandy and rancid.
Sudden explosion

into white silence decades
of quiet could never preclude.
You don't recognize
any world you made

you made him. The stars
no longer above or the ground
bound between covers.
Only the canal

could contrast Baghdad
falling on a station of dead air.
By degrees of the gun he slung,
the belief is lost.

The cause of despair.
You can't see yourself.
You can't see his white
arms, longer than yours.

The Train is White and the Moon is Strong

You would throw yourself
out *there*. To bridge
your window and terrible dreamless
hours to sand.

Nobody together glides
into view. One cannot follow.
But the train is a theme.
It won't stay away.

You miss no ocean,
just the green canal
vanishing in light, continuous.
Nobody told you

to notice, to stretch headlong,
to reach from a theme
of no rain that won't go away.
Hear the train. Take it

into your white arms.
What you're living toward
is unlike time you cannot borrow,
one shore extended.

Roads Over Roads

Duck floats the canal
and calls your light odor
Song Against Washing,
Wash Against Burning,

Poem Over Blackwash.
Under algae a dead stone
road, and this new road's over
where tracks were pulled up.

Alongside the first
thin road crept freight trains,
their men and cargo.
The trees before these.

Your dreams of shrapnel
float over the bank, then
sudden thunder.
Duck under the orange leaves.

A sign warns against
approaching nesting swans
and who would expect
anything but hostility.

Flight-long, Unerring

Inhabit that warmth
and leafy smell, humid
evenings by the sink.
No dead air above

cold water pouring.
The grey road follows
the slow green canal.
He did not vanish but drifted

across; you listen for him
as the train travels
your inner signal, extending
evening, thread of vapor

whose end is morning.
The moon can never be white.
The fox was not white.
His shit car is rust.

Tomorrow's always flight-long,
unerring. His call
dissipates. Or the green canal
reverses its spell.

Spleen Elegy

Little autumn flies in the skein
of southbound geese drowned out
by traffic, an even lower grade season
when I have no change for the meter.
Caffeine combats fatigue, symptom
of anemia the hematologist can't explain.
There is iron in sundown, the approach
of needed rain, clouds filtered
by nothing and cooling an evening
scene out of which optimism is rising.
Here is Pitkin Plaza, three boys
sharing a cigarette, antibodies
bound to platelets that fuzzed-out guitars
in headphones eliminate. Downtown
clouds are dirty enough to breathe.
Anticipating early winter, the barista
concocted me a bittersweet vaccine:
inky and pungent are the grounds
that settle, black as our banter.
Verbatim I'll repeat her practiced smile
of recognition, my beloved habit.
The chill raises my pink seam and I circulate.
Tonight I will dodge no panhandler,
I will deny myself no side street
under a sagging telephone line. Because
a ticket waits on the windshield
I will participate in the economy

of pavement, its rough image of
darkening sky, and for once accept
depth as relative. There is little
autumn in this chunk of broken tar:
worn gray, just smaller than my fist,
and lighter. It's all in my foot-long scar.
I am in the plate glass window
walking with a less pronounced limp
and my left hand not at all idle
as it turns the jagged thing I call rock.
I drop the rock into a storm drain.
Antifreeze, Coca-Cola, runoff,
rain. To resist is to filter. Some particle
will catch as another breaks loose.

Franz Not Your Father

Franz not your father called earlier and left you a message: Difficulty requires consciousness, to which I replied, That is simple to understand and so I will tell her. Often one condition requires another which does not reciprocate. Franz not your father is totally German in his austerity. Our friend's father, whom she had not known since she was seven, died unexpectedly, and a mysterious man with an authentic Albanian name I would never remember called to notify her. I know her less intimately now but that is not the point. I called back Franz not your father and asked if he had seen you, and he replied, I remember the look on your face when you were waking. How could he? To be in the other's company is a mutual room. While I was in the coma I had difficulty breathing, which I forgot to mention, as I was not calling to disprove him, or to request that he define consciousness. There are levels and degrees, each a nuanced description. I told him everything I knew about our Albanian friend whose father twice disappeared and his lack of reply reminded me that he is Franz, which isn't to say nobody's father.

Code

I will blink when you say the word I do not know I am thinking, I will blink until it means you still and sleeping. When you wake with the question, *what did you find on the wet highway where your head shattered glass and you had no speech*, I will blink until it means *yes*. In motion-picture rhythm. A sort of nod. Our code can only be deciphered with steely instinct, an Olivetti typewriter, and a tight-fisted drive into the Brass City to see the last hand-painted sign, in brown and blue, for Timepiece Repair. If I blink rapidly enough for the letters *w*, *r*, *i*, and *t* in *wristwatch* to stop fading, the old man of miniscule tools will come out mouthing the word I am not thinking until you say it. I am blinking in a circle. If you guess then name what the man's been drinking he will not appear so translucent, pencil on onion skin. Obsolete. I lose track of which decade we live in, I indulge my analog craving. Later in the living room repeat the word I am not yet typing, in an angle of sun, and I will blink twenty-four letters per second. Until I am speaking. The slow trees in the clerestory windows sway, almost pixelated.

The Joinery

what we say
approaches

symmetry
therefore works

into a pattern
a design of use

not against
the asymmetrical flame

but the compulsion
of burning

the words offer
a smooth drawer

a slender shelf
sturdy

on tapered legs
sleek profile

of amber teak
holds together

with no hardware
visible

only
mortise and tenon

Polaroid of Former Occupants

under the mat in the closet
we find left behind

the draftsman and a woman
maybe after a party

not quite erotic
not quite casual

if I tell you these strangers
lived to dance then suddenly

they are married
not so random or antique

or even more so
if we dress up like them

green sequined gown
dark blue suit

if we borrow their pose
their repose can you

tell me what they are saying
every name they've ever had

Blank Score

if the weather is not
a key signature

if I am flat on the fire
road without a metronome

if sharp as twilight
I say *snow*

if I repeat a line
through erratic measures of trees

if I finally learn to tell you
about the woodpecker

but give you more
than a transcription

if I learn to listen
will you spot him

hammering
for insects

beak
and echo

The Green Marina

the Green Marina
was not my dream

today I inhabit your copper
planter's evolving

patina and a tomato stalk
rising in open air

the Green Marina
I confess

was where I thought I belonged
one summer

where I belonged
was somewhere to leave

there were boats
I could never own

and only underwater
did the plants flaunt color

I believe in the Green Marina
I could not see

Sky Introduction

A man and a black dog running along
the row of white trees,
the problem begins in spring, the blossoms—

I am parked on an infamous street.

For a year I tried to pick up
where nothing left off. A cross-town road
with no sidewalks or picturesque porches.

I work the clutch weakly—
My crushed left foot fits no shoe.

Putting on boots, dressing the body, is simple.
One limb at a time.

But left and right are matters of direction.

Before sleep I wriggle each arm from its sleeve.
I know little of snakeskin and so

dream of moving low

in the grass. Waking is the row of white trees,
a path of vision
I want my legs to follow. Leading with the left.

I search for invisibility.
Between the limbs blue shapes are shifting.

The black dog is running back.

When Big Joan Sets Up

Imagine having enough left
to break a bottle over it.
Listen how pretty, listen

for glass in nothing nearby
shattering, just morning birds
that do not wake whoever

is not sleeping. Come here
Little Birdie, *come here*.
No matter how great the gains

so many complaints hang—
The grass full of worms,
and still all that squawking,

like a couple talking and talking
about never talking. The chatter
of hunger, that gaudy red—

Bethany Dusk Radio

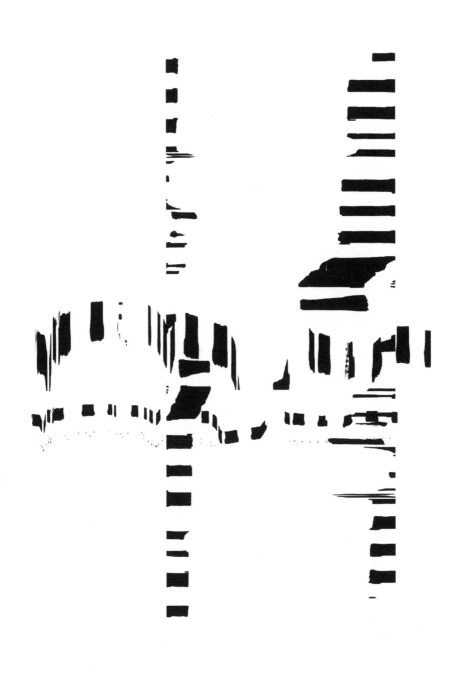

Gap-toothed

Static in the signal, cobalt dusk breaks up in branches
but only one of us believes it. It's difficult
not to feel curious about the temperature
of a higher elevation. Or an estranged city at sea level.

In a minor key we describe a town seen in passing
as a dream embellished in its telling.
Let me tell you everything to know about travel:
somewhere a brown horse is stuck in the mud.

Every low stone wall that snakes across forest
to intersect a smaller property or border
mountain laurel traces back, further and farther.
A single stone wall. A canal digital with interruptions.

Predicting our future location is simple. But
measuring the particulars of compensation is complicated—
if a traumatic accident brings a small fortune
which portion of the ocean evaporates? Then where?

Evening pivots as a key change and withholds
the cymbal crashes, dent in the gas tank. Woodsmoke
and rain find a radius of crushed stone, no cardinal
at the center. My left ear aimed west I listen for a train.

Flung Likeness

Where certain combinations of dusk-light are difficult
Walt Whitman is best experienced
on the molecular level. As vapor, as cloud, as the formation
of objects and animals. All is work and near to everything

here in future conversations. It is difficult to believe in karma
when petty, jealous biomass succeeds. Listen:
conservation of energy, a new mantra: no work is ever
wasted. The snake is furious in its basket of cellular interference.

                    *

As though stone desired placement, your left hand swerves
in hyperbole to suggest *physical labor*. How about nothing else
meriting a series of plaintive questions, exuberance
without action, sound waves propelled into negative space.

The trees are bare so now I can count them. Exposed
just above the brush the low stone wall snakes across acres,
marks out some forgotten grid. You can see across
almost to the other side. In stone a trace

of earlier ice. Consider the uncountable floating particles
as a stick like a broken spoke, virtually soundless
without its connections, washes up in the canal, further
displaced. Pick it up, put your headphones on.

Beginning with a Theme by Joe Brainard

I remember dinners on your fire escape.
I remember a pot of rice falling to the floor.
I remember us riding the subway with a video camera.
I remember trying to predict the future.

Our occasional hostility toward one another
resembled a shore in winter. It was difficult
not to feel curious about the temperature
of the water. Difficult not to touch it.

Walt Whitman, man of rivers and of every transition
ground to ether, bequeathed himself to grow
from my stolen wallet. From fire escapes and water towers,
from F train faces and sidewalk chatter.

As for fashion, black was The New Expensive
before grey was The New Ambivalent.
I kept my pants but changed my shirt.
I dream of money. Whatever...

Everywhere we live with a river on either side,
a world of seas. Only one of us can swim.
Or, we both can swim
but only one of us believes it.

Park Life

Clouds no longer decompose and recompose
objects and animals
when we dream with increasing frequency
of drifting into a blue expanse. A portion of the ocean

and you in all your water will evaporate,
supposedly. A cosmos rarely of water is expanding,
allegedly. From memory sketch kudzu
on the tracks, years-ago Virginia. Listen for a train

in the static. If rate times time equals foothills growing
into mountains, conservation of matter
means no atom's ever wasted—
no woodsmoke, no rain, and still a radius of stone

with us at the center. Do we hear the roof, do we hear rain,
or do we praise a new combination? Afternoon dissolves
and aluminum dusk breaks up, light in clicking branches
we don't have to leave behind to need. Maybe

the city washes away. For now recognize my throwback
to Wu-Tang—I listen and watch for a vixen.
Later allow me to demonstrate not listening for the buck
as I turn off a CGI universe on a plasma screen.

Here and Homeward Bound

Fact is that no machine could kill Pound, only
incite new ideas in sound, in the momentum
of fast rattlers and flat wheelers into negative space.
Windows open, book open—the record is spinning

into a difficult landscape. It is difficult to predict
the particulars of the future, more so to believe in karma,
and it is difficult not to resent the falling temperature
where certain combinations of dusk-light are difficult.

Some animal approaches if you don't listen. After the leaves,
before the leaves, we resent a familiar predicament:
Morning noise floor of dry leaves, no barrier—
that sting in the chest, in the gut, you can't put a thumb on it.

*

Swerve onto a fainter highway, into desert. Dream
the motorcycle before it was seized and spider webs.
With your left hand make a plaintive sort of gesture,
lights flashing. So much of driving is out the window.

Who's behind you. Rate times time equals the ground
growing from hills to ether, sun showers turning into night-
snow, the driver who leads you running out of cigarettes.
Death Valley, the background, not exactly diminishing.

Five Discreet Scenarios with Deep Field Background

So what now. A shape is opening between a café table
and not knowing how to act comfortable,
the right word, the proper gesture
around no stranger. All that weight in negative space.

*

We had to learn where to live, had to pencil ourselves
into a sketchbook of fire escapes and water towers,
a notebook of F train faces and sidewalk chatter.
One's desire is another's dilemma in crosshatching. Illegible snippet.

*

A world of seas only one of us can swim surrounds
the grid of new growth. Of stone we listen for a train.
Midnight and nothing's
green, neither canopy nor shield. Total barrier. The signal blocked.

*

I have something accurate to say that lacks perspective.
I'll bend the note as though to send and then forgive
ancient mistakes—for instance, hyperbole. I'll package and ship you
exuberance for twenty-five cents or acts of physical labor.

*

Never broke, the cosmos contained as it composed
my stolen wallet, everything of star-stuff.
On the molecular level Walt Whitman illuminates
the signal, our midnight vision of a train, atom by atom.

Snake Fire in a Basket Future

cobalt signals a branch breaking up
pine snake stones a forest
woodsmoke crashes   rain withholds
      mountain laurel further back

your left hand swerves near everything
the uncountable floating particles
      wasted the snake in its basket
no work a new mantra

      escape the fire riding a future
the temperature a shore resembled swims
before grey believes Walt Whitman rides
the subway   to grow the new video floor

dream the motorcycle before it was seized
      and spider webs
Virginia listens to years ago
      and you evaporate

pixelate the nocturnal animals
and the music goes gangsta   star-stuff
deserts and diminishes what digital universe
atom   by atom

Lullaby for Bethany

Our former city's transmission crackles
and tells me the time of night is almost forest
The needle catches in the run-out groove
Heavy beat in the trees fades to a loop of dead wax

Real radio absence I forgive beyond midnight
Sleep and rain fade into the past tense
in which my blood dries in the crook
where the road meets the curb

The transmission of the half-dead crackles
and is half-dead
                    the old injury clicking
                    a dry branch ticking

Bethany why are you sleeping so early
Has my asking woken you
Can your nightmare of the woods on fire
occur beyond the molecular level

Don't wake the miles between our bed and the tower's red
Walt Whitman sing us a lullaby
that drowns out the chatter of the near-dead
the jingles for obsolete products and that devil of static

Poem in an Open Tuning

Real radio absence I forgive into morning
snow in the past tense. What would the community
think is what could they.

        Say threshold, say brink, have a preference.

They'll never show you   *the easy way*
the perfect life   *you'll never see*
      guaranteed
      If I was a photographer

How can you fake the Blues Life? Say drink, say
another, then one more and another.
Remember our friend who thought she could
just count to twelve and suffering's red curtain would open?

Who never told you   *you'll never see*
picture taking   *mistaking beautiful*
picture taking   *whose robes did they trade you*
Everyday stage fright floats into the past tense.

My winter once lived in a parking lot. The white van
was a bathysphere snow fell light
across. The van filthy and the radio always on,
it never disappeared. I'd sunk below the surface.

Development is a Threat to Mystery

The transmission of the half-dead crackles
and is half-dead
                    a wet wing clicking
                    a dry branch ticking

I can hardly hear the present over my obsession
with the city where our night is no longer permitted
                    the chatter of a café
                    transmitted this distance

Bethany why are you sleeping so early
Has my asking woken you
Will your nightmare of the woods on fire
                    occur beyond the molecular level

Does your nightmare progress as a vision
a fresh clearing and another piece of
                    the mystique violated
Reception weakens as the dark trails off

I reach and listen to our former city crackle
It tells me the time of night is almost morning
        If something too grotesque crescendos
singer don't let us listen

Highway Sweetheart

Which signal received belies direction and speed?
The stray tone in my ear grows into a song in your head.
We open the window to something heavy, blue note
in the trees. Before long the road along the canal runs out.

The dream is to salvage the motorcycle
and ride deeper into the life-size atlas, the plan
I am drawing for a new and unlivable city
of obsolete electronics and broken guitar strings.

There will be a snare drum with a split head
past a toy xylophone lacking mallets.
There are three Barbies behind microphones,
never in a dumpster or landfill. Blackwash Canal transmits

another color, dream of a westbound highway. Where
that blue signal runs out, find us washed up on a not-so-Californian
shore of digital noise. Do not mistake the sand
for pixels, or the pixels for a seagull discovering

a cracker crumb under a cigarette butt.
You could cover a wall with the postcards.
You could leave the window open and over years
let night sounds blow the colors out.

Variations on Stevens with Primary Colors

Dusk inches in, high-resolution. Images absorb
terabytes of disk space and never mellow the cold of it.
Beyond a blank screen one radio tower blinks
red to another across the valley. Goodbye goodbye goodbye.

Rest comes with the radio on, voices
without faces or in some cases names. They talk you
out of another conversation. Out of your room
with the door hastily shut. What hangs the phone up.

The red voice in absent weather not from under a mask
but like the sea aloft, what evaporated eventually returning.
The grinding water, the rasping wind.
Merely a place, an object, and we sing. Total clouds.

Red absence   on the radio
names the talk   *that* talk
                Your ear canal could carry
yellow signal caught in cloud   a farewell

There is a redder way to say it inside a fading hour
but I don't know a word of it. If I tell you how
transmit all of yellow me while I tilt in a bed of blue.
Red in my ear, in my head, all right all night goodbye.

Notes

"Later in the Black-Eyed Susans" is for the city of Charlottesville, Virginia.

"Waltz for Debby" borrows its title and some themes from the Bill Evans album of the same title. The poem is also inspired by the cover image from the album *Portrait in Jazz*.

"Oar" borrows from Skip Spence's album of the same title and is inspired by the song "Little Hands."

"After Infection" is for Charles Wright.

"Moth Light" borrows its title and some of its materials from the Stan Brakhage film of the same title.

"Spleen Elegy" is for the city of New Haven, Connecticut.

"When Big Joan Sets Up" borrows its title from the Captain Beefheart song of the same title, from the album *Trout Mask Replica*.

"Bethany Dusk Radio" is for Melissa and the town of Bethany, Connecticut. The sequence borrows from, among other songs and poems, Whitman's "Song of Myself," Joe Brainard's book *I Remember*, Cat Power's album *What Would the Community Think*, the songs of Woody Guthrie (as well as the slogan written across his guitar, "THIS MACHINE KILLS FASCISTS"), the Lungfish song "Highway Sweetheart" from the album *Pass and Stow*, and Stevens' poem "The Idea of Order at Key West."

Acknowledgments

Thank you to the editors of the following journals in which these poems first appeared, often in different versions or with alternate titles:

American Letters & Commentary: "Interior Talk Radio," "The Train is White and the Moon is Strong" (from "Return to the Canal");
Boston Review: "If a Train";
Colorado Review: "After Infection," "Half-Life in the Half-Light";
Conjunctions: "Blackwash Canal";
Conjunctions (online)*:* "Waltz for Debby," "Spleen Elegy";
Court Green: "A Reception, a Garage, Mountains North and South";
The Dirty Pond: "Later, in the Black-eyed Susans," "Sky Introduction";
Handsome: "Oar";
Hayden's Ferry Review: "Tattoo Removal";
H_NGM_N: "Bethany Dusk Radio";
The Hat: "The Orgasm as Minor Failure";
Indiana Review: "Blank Score";
Locuspoint: "Solo," "Metal Heart";
Poetry: "When Big Joan Sets Up";
A Public Space: "Moth Light";
Sentence: "Code";
Tarpaulin Sky: "The Joinery," "Franz Not Your Father";
thethe: "Blue Note".

Various poems appear in *Blackwash Canal*, published by H_NGM_N BKS in their portable document format chapbook series.

Boundless love and gratitude to my family, friends, mentors, readers, and fellow musicians, without whom this would be so much less. Thanks to

Melissa. Thanks to Geoffrey Gatza, Melanie Willhide, Dan Beachy-Quick, Darcie Dennigan, Michael Kelleher, Brad Amorosino, and Michelle Lee.

A note on the artwork: The cover and interior images were created specifically for this book by photographer Melanie Willhide, whose recent work is often generated using cheap scanners—modified to the extent of sometimes breaking—in lieu of a camera. She and I have collaborated for many years and share various thematic and aesthetic concerns, particularly the intersection (or collision) of the analog realm with digital technology. I am grateful for her friendship, her body of work, and her contribution to this project.

Jason Labbe's poems, reviews, and nonfiction have appeared widely in such venues as *Poetry*, *A Public Space*, *Boston Review*, *Conjunctions*, *Colorado Review*, *DIAGRAM*, *Ephemeroptera*, *Indiana Review*, *Gulf Coast*, and in a handful of chapbooks, including *Dear Photographer* (Phylum Press) and *Blackwash Canal* (H_NGM_N BKS). A former Henry Hoyns Fellow, he has taught at the University of Virginia, the University of Connecticut, and Southern Connecticut State University. He is also a drummer and recording engineer and has worked with many artists in New England and New York City.

78870427R00062

Made in the USA
Columbia, SC
21 October 2017